I0014676

INSTAGRAM

How to Clarify Your Message and Become an
Expert Influencer Using Instagram

(Build Your Brand, Network Marketing Business
and Instagram Marketing)

Barbara Shelton

Published by Andrew Zen

Barbara Shelton

All Rights Reserved

*Instagram: How to Clarify Your Message and Become an
Expert Influencer Using Instagram (Build Your Brand,
Network Marketing Business and Instagram Marketing)*

ISBN 978-1-989965-84-9

All rights reserved. No part of this guide may be reproduced in any form without permission in writing from the publisher except in the case of brief quotations embodied in critical articles or reviews.

Legal & Disclaimer

The information contained in this book is not designed to replace or take the place of any form of medicine or professional medical advice. The information in this book has been provided for educational and entertainment purposes only.

The information contained in this book has been compiled from sources deemed reliable, and it is accurate to the best of the Author's knowledge; however, the Author cannot guarantee its accuracy and validity and cannot be held liable for any errors or omissions. Changes are periodically made to this book. You must consult your doctor or get professional medical advice before using any of the suggested remedies, techniques, or information in this book.

Upon using the information contained in this book, you agree to hold harmless the Author from and against any damages, costs, and expenses, including any legal fees potentially resulting from the application of any of the information provided by this guide. This disclaimer applies to any damages or injury caused by the use and application, whether directly or indirectly, of any advice or information presented, whether for breach of contract, tort, negligence, personal injury, criminal intent, or under any other cause of action.

You agree to accept all risks of using the information presented inside this book. You need to consult a professional medical practitioner in order to ensure you are both able and healthy enough to participate in this program.

Table of Contents

Introduction

You will see the real tricks they use, how they use other people to help them, and what would typically cost a fortune to complete. Now you'll have the knowledge and the power to do it all by yourself.

Although these are called tips and tricks, they are more actual strategies which social media marketing companies use to achieve the same results. Everything I show is used, and I'll prove they work as you move your way through the information. This title is brief, but full of the **only** vital information you really need to know, and not any fluff that isn't necessary.

One way these secrets are achieved by social media marketing companies is: they create a fake profile which has pictures that grab users' attention, and from this; automated systems are in place to comment on the main pages where the top-rated user has millions of followers. Without knowing, these users are guided to other profiles and pages as well.

This, in turn, raises followers and brand awareness on the main page, and this isn't happening once or twice per day, it happens thousands of times per day. Yes, quite literally.

Chapter 1: Why Is Social Media Important?

It used to be that to market a new brand without a lot of money, you had to take an ad out in the newspaper, and maybe get a cheap commercial on your local television stations. Those were the days where a backyard brand needed a lot of funding to get off the ground. Now it seems even the lowest budgeted marketing strategies get noticed. Why is that? Well, it has to do with the internet taking the world by storm.

Before the days of the internet, sharing something took a lot of foot work, and the time and effort it took to get the word out were not worth it to a lot of people. They sat there with ideas in their head and no way to share them with the world. It is a sad thought really. Can you imagine not being able to share a really cool idea with your best friend because they are too far away? However, that is not a problem anymore, because the internet connects millions of people instantly.

More businesses these days are operating through social media networks. These networks connect them to people around the world. All they have to do is type something one time, and millions of people see it all at once. This is an amazing thing if you think about it, because of just twenty years ago, this was almost unheard of, as the internet was just becoming popular and was very expensive.

However, now it is as easy to obtain as electricity, and ninety percent of households have home internet. Five percent of the households that do not are Amish, or otherwise against modern technology. The other five percent are the families that live below the poverty level. This is how important internet has become in today's society. Schools now have tablets for their students and Wifi for their students to use. Computer labs are no longer big rooms full of windows 98 computers; they are rooms with sleek, thin windows ten computers. Nearly everyone has an account on some social media platform, and many people spend most of their day checking various notifications, and just scrolling if they are not doing anything else.

Social media has become so essential in our daily lives that we are constantly using it to communicate with other people. The older generations often complain that the younger generation spends so much time on the internet talking to people around the world that they forget about the people who are right in front of them. And that can be a problem because it is hard to balance reality and social media, especially when you are trying to run a business from it.

So what exactly is social media? I am pretty sure that everyone uses it, but let's look at it from a technical perspective for a moment. What is social media? It is the platforms in which people share about their lives with people from around the world. They can talk to people from all walks of life about the same things they would discuss at a dinner party. You can keep in touch with old friends who have moved away, and you can meet new ones who live across the nation from you.

Social media started out in its fledgling years on sites such as MySpace. These sites were often frequented by teenagers and were geared to the younger generation to find classmates and keep in touch after high school. However, eventually the adults started getting into the social scene, and many other sites were developed. Nowadays there are social media sites for sharing pictures, posts, mini blogs, dating sites, and much more.

These sites are a great tool for marketers because you can reach a lot of people at one time, and it is entirely free. Unless you choose to boost your posts for a fee, which is still cheaper than taking out an ad in the paper. Marketers are using social media more and more these days because of the ease in which they can share new developments in their companies. This is important because it brings the little guy back into the picture.

The little guy is the guy who is just starting out in a business and doesn't have a lot of financial backers, so finances are tight. There are so many different platforms that you can share with a whole range of people with ease. And this helps the little guy get the word out to the world about his product. He doesn't have to spend a lot of money, in fact, if done right, he can do it for free. This saves him money to put into the product that he is trying to sell to make it the best possible quality.

Social media is not only for people to share things about their life, it is to connect people, and it can also bring them into the spotlight, and get them noticed by people around the world. That is the goal of a lot of people on social media. To get noticed, and become famous. However, some people just use it to keep up with family and friends.

Back a few years ago, if you marketed on social media, it was considered cheap, but now it is the new normal. Everyone does it, from the people selling supplement pills, to someone with a legitimate business looking for employees. There is no end to the people who advertise on social platforms on the internet.

So these are the reasons why social media is important. Not only for marketing but for keeping you connected with grandma when you are traveling abroad, or going to college. It keeps people together, and it is useful for telling multiple people something at one time.

Chapter 2: Creating The Perfect Bio

"Don't bother counting likes, count invoices instead." - Unknown

Before tackling the many Instagram tactics you can use to make sales, there is one thing we must focus on first - your bio. This is your first impression or an elevator pitch for your business and it's a make or break moment. Having a clear, concise and focused Instagram bio immediately makes you look more professional and open for business. New people who find your account will immediately know who you are and what you sell. We live in a day and age where people have short attention spans, they don't want to read a long waffley "about me" page on your website. Your instagram bio has the power to hook in a potential customer with just a few words.

Start your instagram bio with a mission statement summing up what you do or what the product you provide is. It needs to be specific and show people how you can serve them and why they should choose you over any other business. Let's look at some examples of good and bad bios and then see how you can make your own!

Examples for service based entrepreneurs:

• I went from drowning in debt to living a life of abundance and freedom. Now I help other millenial women do the same.

• I help you design custom meals plans that get results and stop you falling off the wagon every three weeks.

• I help women feel confident and beautiful on their wedding day with their dream makeup look.

• Need help with your business? I work with busy mums to turn their side hustle into a full time thriving business.

Examples for product based businesses:

• Activewear designed to inspire and change your life.

• Luxury candles made with love to inspire millenial women.

• It's time to get organised and stop missing those important meetings with our busy women planners.

• Handmade and printed with love in New Zealand - Framed prints to transform your home.

Examples of a BAD bio:

- I help people get fit

- Experienced and qualified accountant

- Makeup artist

- Luxury candles

- 2020 planners and calendars

How do I get there myself?

Sit down and take time to brainstorm your ideal customer. It's not just women - it's their age, what they do for work, if they have a family, how they like to learn, what they do in their spare time, how much money they make etc.

Start with a blank piece of paper and write down all the words that come to mind about your ideal customer and what you want them to get out of your business. Try to think of words that could ignite a feeling in your potential customer or a few sentences that really tell a story about your products.

Ask yourself what are the biggest struggles or needs for your client? Then write down how you can solve those problems. Finally, summarise how you solving that problem will change their life.

I recommend service based entrepreneurs use the "I help" statement/method. The structure works like: I help [audience/customer] overcome [insert pain point/struggle] so they can [overall goal]. Alternatively, you can use the "past/present" method structured like: I went from [past point] to [present point] and now I help [target audience/customer] do the same.

While for product business, make sure you are using words that spark emotion and connection. You don't just sell activewear - you are selling clothes that help women find the confidence to change their lives. Think beyond just your simple product. I don't have a specific formula for product businesses as it depends a lot on the item you are selling, but use the brainstorming techniques above and you will find something that will be effective.

It may seem like a lot of effort for one small sentence in your bio, but trust me it's important. It will also continue to help you when you might feel lost some days about where to take your business. Unsure what to write for a caption or what to post on your stories? Go read your Instagram bio for some inspiration and reinforce the clarity on what your business is all about. We will also discuss more on writing captions in chapter 4!

Top tip:

A lot of my clients find me by searching "social media managers" on the Instagram explore page. So how am I getting my account to show up first ahead of other agencies that possibly have more followers? My instagram username is @ellenmackenziee but my actual 'name' under my account isn't Ellen Mackenzie - it's "Ellen - Social Media Manager". Having this keyword or job title in my name means my account shows up when people search for a social media manager. This has been a fantastic and very simple way to get new clients. Try brainstorm some keywords that aren't about your specific products, programs or business but are words that you think your ideal client might be searching. But of course, you still need to have the beautiful bio and fantastic content on your page to really hook in the new follower and get them to make a purchase. Which brings us to the next chapter - making a connection with your customer!

Chapter 3: Starting Your Instagram Presence

Social media is one of the best ways to reach your target audience. It seems like everyone is on social media now and the companies that refuse to have any sort of presence on these sites are the ones who usually see a large decrease in their customer base. There are many social media sites that you can choose from and with a little bit of research, you will be able to find the one that has most of your target audience and use this to your advantage.

One of the social media sites that you may want to consider is Instagram. This is one of the most popular social networking sites and it is pretty simple to use and can showcase your business in many different ways. This social media site is going to allow you to share any video or photo that you would like with the potential to reach people all throughout the world. Many individuals choose to go on Instagram and use it to show what they are doing and to keep up with friends and family. But it can really provide some unique ways to showcase your business by showing off your service or product.

Think about the many ways that you would be able to use Instagram to boost your business. You can create videos that could go viral, put pictures up of new products, and share information in ways that are not possible with some of the other social network sites.

Posting on Instagram is the easy part, though. Like with other social networking sites, you will find that gaining some fans on Instagram can be tough, especially if you are new. Some businesses try to get dominance in this site by working on spam as well as other inappropriate content, but this is often going to make people annoyed with your page and you will start to lose some of the customers that you want. There are several options that you can choose from that will help you to find fans, fans who are there because they like your product or because they have purchased it in the past. Some of these options include:

Figure out what aspect you should focus on

When you want to do some marketing of your business with the help of Instagram, you need to figure out what you want to focus on. Many times beginners will want to try and dabble in everything and they hope that these activities will catch on so that others will start to follow them. This approach is not really a great idea because you are all over the place and really just wasting your time. So instead of trying to offer everything to your customers, choose one aspect and then concentrate on that one aspect.

Let's look at an example of how this would work. Say that you were creating an Instagram account in order to show off some of your painting skills. Here you will need to focus on just your skills in painting so make sure that all of the videos and photos that you work on should just show this skill. Yes, there are a lot of great memes and videos out there that are pretty popular, but they aren't really helping to promote the painting part of the business and if you add in all of those other things, you are just confusing your customers.

Remember that you are a business so you should be concentrating on your business. Unless you are a celebrity or you are using Instagram as your personal site, you should not update your customers on all your daily activities or post other things that have nothing to do with your business. Your customers are going to be there because they enjoy what you have to offer in services and skills, not because they want to know what you are having for supper.

Change the appearance of the account

After you pick out the focus that you want to work with, it is time to change around the appearance that goes with your account and make it look better. You should start out with a good profile picture as well as a good and thoughtful description that can help out with this task. This is a good start, but you need to do more if you want to stick out. It is important that you also secure the look of the photo feed of the account.

A simple way that you can do this is to collect about twenty pictures that go along with your chosen focus. This is going to be your portfolio and it should have some higher quality images. Make sure that if you have been using the Instagram page before that you get rid of all the stuff that is irrelevant or unattractive from the page. The photo feed in your page is a great way to attract others to the page so make sure that you are able to take high quality and interesting pictures or have someone else do it for you.

Share the Instagram page

Sometimes the best way to make sure that people are able to find your Instagram account is to share it with others. You can start with some of your other social networking sites, especially if these are better established for your business. Starting with Google+, Twitter, and Facebook, you can work through some of your social media sites and let others know that you have the Instagram account available.

In addition, if you have some marketing materials for your business or you have an email contact list of customers, you can send information about your Instagram to them. Some of them may be really interested in following you to find out more about the business, your promotions, and your products and services and this can be a great way to get ahold of some of your customers who may not be using the other sites you are on.

Interact on Instagram

By going through your existing network, you may be luck enough to get some great Instagram followers, but it is important to keep on working from here. If you are only dealing with your current fan base, you are not going to be getting anyone new and you won't see the growth that you want form your business. One thing that you are ale to do in order to get some of these followers is to interact with some of the other users on Instagram and search through their followers to see who is in their potential audience.

You need to make the interactions with the other Instagram users look as normal as possible; otherwise, it is going to show up as spam inside of the system. For example, don't use too many hashtags in the work, don't ask the user for a shout out, and don't do any exchanging of follows and likes. They were once effective when Instagram was brand new, but they are just not effective any longer.

The most effective method that you can use in order to get the attention of the user is to comment on a video or a photo that they uploaded. Make sure that the comment is positive and thoughtful, something that is more than a few words. You should leave your actual thoughts about the content and say something that will grab their attention. If you write out something that is thoughtful and that others will enjoy, you are more likely going to get others back to your page. Never write out that you want others to follow your account, though; this is seen as spam and will turn many potential fans away.

Engage the followers

Once you have some of the followers that you want on your page, it is not enough to just have them there, you need to be able to engage them as well. If you take these followers for granted and don't keep up with them, you will start to lose them. It doesn't have to be a lot of work to engage the fans and customers, though. You just need to make sure that the page is getting regular updates, that you are answering questions and comments that your fans place on, and put new videos and pictures up on a daily basis.

Remember with this one that the quality is going to be better than quantity. Posting too many pictures and videos all the time will just annoy some of your followers so keep it down to just the ones that are high quality and try to spread them out to different times during the day to catch fans when they get on. Keeping the pictures and posts to no more than one per a six-hour period will help.

Increasing your presence on your Instagram account is one of the first steps that you will need in order to make more people see about your business. You can always start with some of the fans that you have from other pages, but interacting with some other pages that are similar to yours and making your page look really nice and on topic can help you to really bring in some of those fans that will make your business do better.

Getting More Followers without Having to Spend Money

Now that we have some ideas on how to establish a presence online for your business with the help of Instagram, it is time to work on how to increase your followers. You also need to learn how to expand out some of your networking so that you can find some more followers. Unfortunately, when most beginners start looking at methods of doing this, you will find that the first methods that show up will cost you a lot of money. You can choose to go with one of these "Instagram experts" if you would like to spend a lot of money, but often a new business is on a tight budget and these experts can be overpriced sometimes.

In this chapter, we are going to take a look at some of the techniques that you can use in order to grow some of that fan base without having to spend a whole lot of money. The major advantage of these is that they actually work without having to hire the experts and hope that they work. Some of the techniques that you can try out include:

Pick the right time to post. Experts state that posting either at two in the morning or five in the afternoon are the best time periods to post your content and be seen by the highest amount of people.

Use the filters on any of your marketing campaigns for Instagram. Some of the most recent reports show that "Mayfair" is a great filter for a marketer to use on Instagram.

Include a lot of information on the bio of the account. This is not the time or the place to get lazy. You need to make sure to use a lot of information here so that the visitors know what you are all about. Add in some keywords and hashtags as well as the URL of your site. This helps interested users be able to access the website of your business easy if you set it up this way.

Pick out some hashtags that your followers will like. These are always changing so you need to make sure that you check up on this and find the ones that your customers will like.

Figure out the target audience that you would like to use and make sure to target them. This means to find and like their pictures, make comments, and interact them. This is a great approach to use when you want to find some of the best followers.

Hold a contest on Instagram. Most businesses by promoting their event with an image and then they will ask some other users to join in this contest by liking the image. This increases your reach quite a bit if it gets popular and you only have to pay the costs of whatever you are giving away.

Offer some coupons, sneak peeks, and other specials that are offered on Instagram and show them to your Facebook and Twitter followers.

Make sure that you are concentrating on photos that are high quality. Low-quality pictures are going to be a big turn off. You should also consider placing these pictures on Wednesdays because this one is a good day for post engagement.

Pictures that have faces in them are often more popular compared to those that don't have faces so try to do this.

Try to make some relationships happen between you and some of the more influential users on Instagram. This makes it easier for some of the customers that you want to find you and be able to follow you later on. Make sure this is a positive relationship, where you often show up and comment and like some of their posts.

Hold a marketing campaign with some of the other Instagram users. There are often other businesses who are complimentary to your industry and the two of you will be able to work together, with similar promotions helping each other out, to increase your business.

Tag some other people in your pictures. There are two advantages that come from doing this. It is going to first display these pictures in the Instagram feed of the person and it is going to help make it more likely that the photos will be shared.

It is also important to spend some time on the pictures that you are using and sharing on your site. You want them to be high quality, picking out ones that your users are sharing, add something inspirational to them, or make some changes so that they tell a story and look nice. Good pictures can help to attract the people that you want while the bad pictures can turn them away.

These are just some of the methods that you can use in order to take your Instagram account and attract some of the viewers that you want. While there are some experts that will charge you a lot of money in order to create your marketing campaign, there are a few things that you are able to do on your own that will help to grow your website and helps you to get the fans and the sales that you want. Keep in mind that this does take a little bit of time, you have to do some of these things consistently over the long term rather than just hoping that it happens overnight, but if you are able to do this, it is easier to get the results that you want.

Chapter 4: Instagram Advertising's Best Tips

Since its inception, Instagram has grown into a community that has become difficult for advertisers to ignore. With millions of users online daily, Instagram has become among the leading social media networks around. A study conducted in 2017 by eMarketer revealed that Instagram's global mobile ad revenues alone will amount to more than 2.5 billion dollars, which is at least 10% more than Facebook's global ad revenue projection. That is incredibly impressive, and for a business, it spells potential that is simply too hard to ignore.

Instagram's popularity and potential have become so hard to ignore that if you're not on the platform, you're losing out as a business. There are thousands of businesses already on the social media platform, eagerly tapping into all its resources to drive their sales figures and lure in potential new customers. Because it has proven to be such a powerful tool, it has cemented a name for itself as being a top marketing channel that businesses everywhere need to effectively reach their audience.

Best Practices to Maximize Your Instagram Ad Potential

Why has Instagram grown to become the advertising phenomenon that it is today? For one thing, it is because it is easier than ever for a brand to sell their products and service on the social media platform. They know for a fact that this is where users are spending a lot of their time, so this is where they need to be if they want to be seen. Why continue advertising the conventional way when nobody is paying attention? You need to go where your consumers go, and that is social media platforms.

Millennial consumers especially prefer online shopping more than anything else, which is why they make up a large percentage of the social media platform's user base. The convenience that comes with online shopping is a huge incentive, and when these consumers are easily able to reach out and contact the brand, that motivates them even more because of the customer service experience that they receive. If your brand is not already advertising on Instagram, you need to get on board and do it quick! Every second that you're not on the social media platform is another second which is wasted because you could have been improving your brand awareness and driving sales. When Instagram was introduced back in 2015, it drove an impressive one billion users and more to take action. These numbers, for a business, means everything.

While there is no sure-fire guarantee that your ads are going to be a massive, roaring success, there are things which you could do to help increase your chances. Start by employing some of these strategies below:

Using the Power of Visuals: Images which are a combination of both powerful and natural are going to be your best bet for this social media platform. Fantastic photos are what Instagram is all about. If you want to bring in the sales, boost your brand's reputation and grab the attention of new customers, high-quality images are going to have to be your mantra. Not just images, but high-quality video content too. Anything that is blurry or pixelated is a big fat no on your Instagram profile. Never compromise on the quality of the visuals. Your images should also "blend in" as part of your Instagram profile, so they look as natural as possible without looking too much like an ad (even though it is). Audiences these days are not about the hard sell anymore, they want something that is genuine and authentic to look at.

Go Easy on the Branding: Linking back to the point above, you want your visuals for both images and video on Instagram to look as authentic and as natural as possible. While you do need to feature your brand and logo on every content your produce, you need to go easy on it and do it in a subtle manner so it doesn't appear like a "direct sales pitch" or hard sell. A good rule of thumb to follow is that your branding should not be overshadowing your product. If it is, then you probably need to scale back on the branding a little bit.

Familiarizing Yourself with the Various Ad Types: You need to know what you're dealing with if you want a successful ad campaign at the end of the day. Otherwise, you're going to be navigating blindly through the social media platform, just hoping for the best and not fully maximizing your ad campaign's true potential. The four main groups of ad types that are the most effective on Instagram include photo ads, video ads, carousel ads, and marquee ads. Marquee ads are one-day campaign ads which guarantee impressions and top ad positions on Instagram's news feed. Marquee ads showcase a business's creativity, because it shows variations of the ad to the same audience group, and this can happen up to three times a day.

Go Easy on the Texts: Instagram is all about the visuals, which means that the less text you have on your post, the better. The more natural your ads look, the more engagement you're likely to receive. Instagram is where your brand's creative powers come to shine, and if you observe some other ad campaigns by other popular Instagram accounts, you will notice that there is hardly any text involved. Instagram's algorithm knows that any content which is too text heavy is not going to reach the large audience that you are hoping for, so it is unlikely that your content is going to get the viewership that you're hoping for.

Keep It Short, Short, Short: Social media, as a general rule, is a fast-moving platform. Instagram is no different. Audiences can spend only seconds on an image or video before losing interest and moving onto the next. On Instagram, if your content is not short, you're not going to win. In fact, on this platform more than any other is where audiences **don't** want to do a lot of reading. They come here for the visuals and the videos. If they wanted to read, they would go elsewhere to do it. Instagram is the ideal example of a platform where less is more in this case, especially when it comes to texts and words. Keep your content to a maximum of 40 characters and nothing more (it's okay if it's less).

Doing a Test Run: This is one way of knowing whether your ads are working the way you intended them to or not. Here's the thing you need to remember, even though you may be managing several different social media platforms, and running the same ad campaign on all of them, you still want to avoid copying and pasting your content. You should also do a test run of your ads before committing to spending money boosting that post. Run a couple of "test ads" on your Instagram stories and profile to see how your audience responds to it. Do they like your content enough to engage with it? Or is it not getting the response that you hope for at all? If it is the latter, it might be worth reconsidering if you'll want to spend money on this campaign. You might have to tweak and adjust your ad a little if it isn't working quite as you hoped. Doing a test run will save you advertising dollars and you don't end up wasting it on content which isn't working anyway.

A Call to Action Is a Must: This goes without saying because, without a proper call to action, your audience is not going to know what needs to be done next. The whole reason you're running this advertising campaign in the first place is that you want to see some real sales results, and if you miss out on the very important call to action, that isn't likely to happen. A call-to-action prompts and reminds your audience about the next step which needs to be taken, and it usually consists of just two words. Shop now, sign up now, apply now, contact us now, watch now, download now and more, depending on the nature of your campaign, can be powerful prompts that encourage the audience to take some action.

Responsive Landing Pages Are a Must: There is nothing more off-putting to the audience that to arrive at a landing page which isn't working. You would have wasted all your time crafting the perfect ad campaign, covering all your bases but only to disappoint and fall short if your landing page is completely non-functional. Just like that, you would have lost the audience you worked so hard to get. To your audience, it is akin to going to the movies and purchasing your ticket, only to be told that your movie has been canceled. Imagine the disappointment. Poor customer service is something which must be avoided at all costs. Always test to make sure your landing pages are in working order so no one is left disappointed at the end of the day.

Getting Seen by the Right People: Once again, the importance of targeting your audience is brought into the spotlight. You've put in all that work into your ad campaign, why waste it all if it isn't going to be seen by the right people. Audiences are the life-force of your ad campaign, without them, your business would flounder really quick. As eager as you are to start getting your ad campaign up and running, it would be wise to spend some time having a real think about who it is you want to put your ad in front of and how you are going to ensure that this happens effectively.

Facebook and Instagram Are **Not** One and the Same

They may be running on the same ads manager platform, because Facebook does own Instagram, but there is a very distinct difference between these two. Even though the integration between Instagram and Facebook is seamless, but from an advertising perspective, they are not the same. One of the distinctive differences between the two is the user-behavior patterns and the demographics involved.

Instagram's demographics consists of a much younger audience, whereas in terms of user behavior, the content which is shared on Facebook is a lot more mixed compared to that of Instagram. Facebook's content can vary from anything to status updates, videos, pictures, memes and more, whereas Instagram is more focused on visuals and videos only. To maximize your ad potential, you must know how to customize your content according to the social media platform's capabilities. Another example of how different Instagram and Facebook are is that Instagram relies heavily on hashtags to spread their content, while Facebook does not. In fact, hashtags simply look odd on Facebook and out of place. Which again emphasizes why each ad must be crafted to suit the platform in question.

Chapter 5: Strategy With Instagram

Instagram, like many of today's social media platforms, offers businesses, big and small, the incredible opportunities to reach both massive audiences, as well as a targeted audience to connect with them, engage them, and ultimately convert them into customers. However, the more brands that join Instagram, the bigger the competition, and the harder it is to stand out in a person's feed. Instagram opened up its new ad feature in 2015, utilizing the Facebook advertising system. With this, marketers can now reach a niche segment of the population, which is currently at 800 million users and growing. Instagram ads have become an avenue for brands looking to increase their engagement and, by extension, their profits, to the 500 million active users who use Instagram every day. In this chapter, you will learn the basics of Instagram ads. We will go through the "what" and the "whys" of Instagram ads, so you have a firm foundation to get you started on creating ads, measuring performance, and improving your ad results.

Why Use Instagram Ads?

Since launching its ad platform in 2015, Instagram has driven more than one billion user actions to date. Just last year alone, advertising dollars have doubled, and its advertiser base, which began at only a few thousand, is now at 500,000 advertisers.

In 2016, a survey by Strata found that 63 % of U.S.-based ad agencies included Instagram advertising into their marketing budget for both their own companies and that of their clients, as well. This is a significant jump from the year before, which showed that only 34 % of advertisers chose to include Instagram advertising into their marketing arsenal. This makes Instagram the most popular choice for advertising. It's not only that. About 60 % of Instagram users are under 30. By 2019, agencies estimate that Instagram will make close to 7 billion in profits through worldwide cellphone ad revenue, thus increasing the profit share of their parent company, which is Facebook's global ad revenues.

Five Reasons to Use Instagram Ads

If you have not started exploring Instagram ads and you think it is worth it, here are a few reasons to help you understand its benefits:

Instagram has a vast audience growth. 26,965 brands were looked at by TrackMaven across all industries, and they found that brands witnessed a 100 percent median follower growth from 2016 to 2017. This shows that Instagram is among the fastest-growing social media platform to date.

Instagram receives a lot of attention from its users. On a daily average basis, users spend a total of 50 minutes on Facebook, Facebook Messenger, and Instagram. In North America alone, an average of one in 5 minutes is spent on browsing Instagram or Facebook.

Instagram can generate intent from its users for the ads they run. In 2016, Instagram conducted a study and found that 60 percent of users mentioned that they have learned about a product or service via Instagram. At least 75 percent said they took part in an action, whether it was telling a friend, purchasing a product, visiting a site, or searching for information after they saw something on Instagram.

Instagram can target specific audiences for their ads. Instagram and Facebook share the same advertising system, although their algorithms may be slightly different. Both Facebook and Instagram have the most potent targeting ability, which means that marketers can specify their target audience based on demographics, location, behavior, interests, and search data. You can also target users based on their interactions with other sites and profiles.

Instagram can produce desirable results for its corporate and business users. There was another survey conducted by Instagram that looked at over 400 campaigns worldwide in ad recall. The study found that Instagram's ad recall was 2.8 times higher than that of other online advertising channels. The types of ads that Instagram offers are around five in terms of ad formats. These are Photo ads, Video ads, Carousel ads, and Canvas Story ads, among others. All these ads are available for you to use toward your target audience's feeds and stories, enabling a smooth user experience while you browse and explore Instagram. These are also available in your Facebook Ad manager, so marketers can utilize Facebook's user data that enable targeting at a precise level. Let us explore the various ads in the next section of this chapter.

The Different Types of Ads to Use in Instagram

Photo ads can be one of the best ways to tell your story, whether it be your business or your brand. It is, in fact, top-notch visual content with even more people. When it comes to using photos, there is no room for bad, low-resolution images. If you want to stand out and be seen, you need to have a distinctive look and feel for your photos that mirror your brand. You also need it to display your product beautifully and authentically, and these photos need to be consistent with your branding guidelines and look and feel. Photo ads also enable marketers to target a particular age group. With the latest updates on Instagram ads, marketers can also include call-to-action buttons, such as "Apply Now," "Book Now," "Call Now," "Contact Us," "Get Directions," "Learn

More," "Get Showtimes," and "Download Video."

Video Ads

These come equally in terms of the most favored content on Instagram. According to data by Instagram, the time spent watching videos is more than 80 %, and videos were posted more than four times in 2017 compared to 2016. The year 2019 is now even a great time for brands to gain on this fantastic way to capture the user's attention. When making videos, you need to make sure that you feature your brand first thing in the video, as it is the best way to get recognized.

Why do this? The answer is so your audience will recall your brand once the video is over. Your video on Instagram should not be longer than 1 minute or 60 seconds simply because the user's attention is not that long to begin with. People want to get to the point fast, and you need to give them an idea of this, at least in the first 5 seconds of the video. A reliable video does not need to be long; 15 seconds will usually be enough. Just like photo ads, there are call-to-action buttons that can be included, as well. These are: Apply Now, Book Now, Call Now, Contact Us, and Download Stories.

Carousel Ads

The unique thing about carousel ads is that it allows users to swipe through a series of videos or images. And there is a call-to-action button that connects them directly to your website or blog. Carousel ads offer brands the uniqueness to tell a story that is longer to their audience, and this will allow them to get into multiple products, share different perspectives, or dive into a single service in a combination of videos or images. Carousel ads work great for exercise and fitness profiles, recipe and food profiles, and even makeup and travel.

Like the other ads, carousel ads can also be targeted to a specific segment if you want to show the versatility of your content or to show various creative assets, such as fashion, food, and design. The call-to-actions that carousel ads support are Apply Now, Book Now, Contact Us, Call Now, and Download Stories.

Stories

These bring a whole new dimension to Instagram ads. Instagram users view Instagram Stories daily; this represents a massive amount of audience that you can reach with it. The only difference with Stories is that it expires after 24 hours. But you can keep them as your profile Highlight if you want to. This is an ideal format to use when you have limited-time offers, promotions, and seasonal discounts you wish to promote. Another great thing about Instagram Stories is that if your account has at least 10K subscribers, you can also add a link to your Stories, so your audience can swipe up when they want to find out more from your website, blog, or YouTube channel. Stories enable brands to go a little crazy by adding face filters, texts, gifs, and effects to create fun and creative promotions. The call-to-action that can be used with your Stories using the swipe-up feature include Apply Now, Book Now, Contact Us, Call Now (video only), and Download Story.

Facebook Canvas

Facebook Canvas is another immersive video format ad for Instagram Stories specifically optimized for mobile use. It loads quickly for a smoother viewing experience. On Facebook, there are plenty of Canvas templates that make it easy for you to build a Canvas ad that suits your needs for Instagram. Companies can choose one of these ad templates or create their custom Canvas for a unique ad experience. These templates enable you to use a combination of videos and photos to showcase variety. These templates are great if you want to show a range of products and include a campaign video. The supported call-to-action buttons that can be added in canvas ads are Apply Now, Book Now, and Contact Us.

Now that you know the different kinds of ads on Instagram that you can use, you are now ready to explore more about Instagram ads and put these ads into practice.

How to Advertise on Instagram

This is a brief to give you an idea of how advertising on Instagram works. We will explore, at a deeper level, how you can create, build, and publish your ads so that they become successful and worth the money you invest in. Essentially, to create ads on Instagram, all you need to do is connect your Instagram account to your Facebook Business Page manager. This allows you to use the Facebook Ad Manager, where you can create ads that run on both Instagram and Facebook or just one of the accounts. The choice is yours.

What if I do not have a Facebook account? While it is possible to open an Instagram account with a Facebook account (you can easily create your Instagram profile with your email address), you can't create ads without a Facebook account. This is because, to create an ad on Instagram, you would need to connect your Instagram account to your Facebook Business Page to use Facebook's Ad Manager. Besides, it is much easier if you had a Facebook account because you would be able to grow and build your audience on both platforms. But because Facebook and Instagram are connected and if you want to push your brand to your target audience, then having both accounts would make sense for your business.

The Ad Manager lets you build and create ads to run on both Instagram and Facebook, or you can choose to run it on either platform. You can also customize your target audience, make payments, monitor the ad's progress, as well as work on other features on the manager. If you already have a Facebook Page, here is how you can connect it to your Facebook Ad Manager. First, visit business.facebook.com. Click on Create Account. Enter a name for your business, select the primary Page, and enter your name and work email address. Enter all the necessary details requested on the onboarding flow. Once you are done setting up, you can then link your Instagram account to your Business profile.

Here is how you can do it: Go to your Business Manager. Look on the left side of the Page for Business Settings. Click on it and click again on Instagram Accounts.

Click Create New Instagram Account.

Add your username and password, then click Next.

To authorize one or more of your ad accounts to use the Instagram Account, check the box next to each ad account and click Save Changes.

If you are unsure whether Instagram ads would benefit your business, the best thing you can do at the end of this book is to give it a try anyway and see how your customers respond to your ads. Having an online account and social media platform for your business means that you have customers looking at you on the Internet.

Furthermore, this means that they are already interacting with other brands and ads on social media. So, whether you are a B2C or a B2B business, Instagram advertising will benefit your brand, as long as you have customers online. Getting started with Instagram marketing and advertising is secure, and this book will help you make it a smooth-sailing process. All you have to do right now is link your Facebook Business Manager. And you are already on the right path.

With an impressive 95 million daily posts (according to Hootsuite) and 25 million registered business profiles (also from Hootsuite) and counting, Instagram advertising is poised to take over the world. This photo-sharing and video-sharing social media platform has dramatically changed the marketing game for businesses, opening up a world of possibilities and new ways for businesses to connect with their clientele. Companies have been able to dramatically connect with their audiences, engage with their target demographics, and drive sales like never before. This is all thanks to the power of social media. About 80 % of Instagrammers (according to Hootsuite) on the platform are actively following at least one business profile.

Define Your Goals

This social media platform is highly competitive, but this also provides a unique opportunity for businesses to engage with their followers. How does a brand stand out successfully? The answer is by doing more than publishing just pretty pictures and the occasional video. For a brand to call its advertising efforts successful, it must develop a well-defined, creative, and detailed advertising strategy. This can only be done if a brand has a clearly defined set of advertising goals that can produce measurable results. Let us start by defining your goals. A lot of businesses, especially the new ones, sometimes struggle with this aspect. Defining goals is not as easy as it may seem. It is not just about saying our goal is to have as many followers as possible because a goal needs to be specific. The more detail you are, the better your marketing and advertising strategy will be. If you are struggling to figure out how to get started in defining your advertising goals, try starting with these questions:

Why did you decide to use Instagram for your business?

How do you believe this platform will help with achieving your overall marketing and business goals?

What is the specific advertising budget you will be able to commit to this platform?

How much time can you commit to advertising on this platform daily?

In what way is Instagram different compared to your other social media platforms?

What does success mean to you?

What are you primarily using this platform for? Do you want to connect with your target demographic better? Or do you aim to build greater brand awareness? To develop higher brand loyalty, perhaps? Is this platform a way in which you offer customer service?

What sort of content do you intend to advertise? Is that content focused on educating your target audience about your business? There could be a long list of reasons and rationales for using Instagram and why you think this method of advertising is going to best help your business meet its goals. As long as you are able to define each reason in detail clearly, you are off to a good start. The advertising goals that you set will have a massive influence on the kind of metrics that you will use to track the success of your efforts, so that is something you might want to keep in mind. Confused? Let us clear that up for you real quick. Let us say you were using Instagram as a platform to engage with your audience as one of your advertising goals, then the metrics you would be using to track that success would be engagement metrics. Engagement metrics involves analyzing the number of comments, likes, and shares that a post receives.

So, how do you start defining your goals? Once you have sorted out your reasons (specific reasons) for choosing this platform, you are now ready to move onto phase two of the goal-setting process.

To start setting active advertising goals, here are the things that you would need to do:

Define your target audience. Who are you aiming to target through this platform? If you have already got a good idea of the demographic you are going after, an excellent strategy to employ would be to start customer profiling. This will give you a better sense of what kind of content your target is after, the sort of hashtags they use, and even what communities they belong to on Instagram. Think of this stage as your due diligence. The more information and details you can gather to create your customer persona, the more definitive your advertising strategy will be.

Define your objectives. The first question you should ask is, "What does your business hope to achieve by advertising on Instagram?" What can you do on Instagram that you cannot compete with other social media platforms? How does this platform integrate with your other social media platforms and marketing strategy? Ideally, your objectives should try to increase brand awareness among your target audience, showcase your brand and company culture, shine the spotlight on your products and services (and why they are different), increase audience engagement, and inspire brand loyalty. Your objectives should also seek to build a more engaged community, connect your brand with both audiences and influencers, increase sales by driving traffic to your site, and more. Your objectives will be the ones to help you navigate and decide on the next course of action.

Have clear guidelines for your team. If there is a team of people involved in helping you run your Instagram advertising efforts, it will help if everyone was clear on what they are responsible for. Guidelines help to ensure that everyone is working in the right direction toward achieving your advertising goals.

Conduct an Instagram audit. This step helps you constructively observe your profile. It is time to take a good, hard, critical look at it. An audit must be done to see if your profile is meeting your business needs, and if it is not, you should know what can be done about it. This step gives you a sense of where you should be focusing your advertising efforts on. Your audit needs to tie in tightly with your goals because every measure that you take should be leading you one step toward achieving the goals that you have set for your brand.

Examples of Advertising Goals and Objectives

Throughout your time on Instagram, your business goals will shift and change according to your business needs. As you accomplish one goal, a new purpose could come in its place, and the key to successful advertising on Instagram is learning how to identify which goals will be complemented by the right kind of advertising objectives. Here are some examples to give you an idea of how to get started.

Building Brand Awareness (Goal): To achieve this goal, the accompanying advertising increases your reach and engagement by boosting your posts. For example, you could create a business ad that is aimed at the people closest to your business vicinity and try to reach as many people as possible. Creating ads that help your audience understand the value of your brand is an excellent way to start increasing brand awareness, especially among new customers.

Target Potential Customers (Goal): Suitable advertising objectives to help you achieve this goal could include increasing website conversion and lead generation by collecting relevant information from individuals (newsletters, new signups, etc.). Objectives could also include how to raise engagement by creating the right kind of ads to help market your events and how to communicate those ads effectively to your target audience group.

Increasing Sales (Goal). Advertising goals that can help you achieve this include creating ads with coupons, one-time offers, or special discounts to increase engagement. Encourage existing Instagrammers to get in touch with you through your app (to encourage more app downloads and participation), creating ads that spark conversation and help your brand better communicate with your audience.

Tips to Run Your Own Successful Instagram Audit

Conducting an audit is so important because it helps you consistently check that your strategy and goals are on track the way that they should be. Take the review as an opportunity to help you reassess your business and your advertising goals. After all, you want to make sure that all that blood, sweat, tears, and countless hours that you are spending on your branding is all worth it in the end and helps your business's bottom line.

Here's how you can run an audit of your Instagram.

Are your KPIs and goals on track? How are you going with your advertising and marketing goals so far? Do your current business goals line up with your advertising goals? Are they working to complement each other? The purposes do not necessarily have to be the same, but they do need to work together to support your overall business goals directly.

What are your business voice and branding like? Does your Instagram have a look, sound, and feel to it that is consistent? Is your branding showing clearly on your profile? Does your Instagram look and feel like the rest of your social media channels? What you are aiming for is for an Instagrammer to be able to come to your profile, take a quick look, and almost instantly be able to get a feel of what your brand is like and what you offer.

How are your aesthetics and content shaping up? Content must be consistent. Consistency of your brand's story is the key to advertising success on Instagram. Your audience must know that you are still active and that your business is still active. If your profile is only updated once a week or once every other week, your followers are going to quickly lose interest because nothing is exciting or interesting enough to remind them that your business is here, that it still exists.

Content and Hashtags

Curate and plan your profile's content carefully, and you will see how quickly it can transform from ordinary to incredible. How well are you engaging with your followers? Are you having the right amount of two-way conversation with your audience the way that you should be? Do your followers feel like your brand genuinely cares for its customers? Do you respond within a reasonable amount of time to the direct messages or comments that you receive on your profile? If you are not doing any of this, your advertising efforts might as well be a waste. It is never going to be as effective as you want it to be without the right kind of audience engagement. No comment should be left unanswered, and no direct message should be left without answering it. Every time someone on Instagram takes the time or effort to either mention or contact you, reciprocate it. No exceptions.

Are you using hashtags? Love them or hate them, hashtags are here to stay. A post with a hashtag included gets an average of 12.6 % more engagement than a position that comes without a hashtag. Which one do you want to be? The answer is the former. The questions you need to ask yourself are whether your business is using the relevant hashtags (are they related to your audience). Are you using a hashtag that is unique to your brand and used consistently, or are your hashtags too generic, which is causing your business to get lost in a sea of thousands of other posts with similar hashtags?

Chapter 6: How To Create An Effective Instagram Marketing Strategy

Millions of people globally are now using Instagram. Instagram has made it easier to take pictures and share them with friends and many people enjoy doing this. Apart from networking, you can use Instagram in a more efficient way of marketing. Instagram is a great promotional tool you can use to promote your business online.

1. Tell the story using photos and videos

Photos are worth a thousand words and Instagram is all about pictures. If you are on Instagram for marketing purposes, then you ought to understand that random photos do not work. You need to post pictures of your product constantly. Posting pictures of your products is one of the best ways of increasing your brand awareness and boost sales of your products. The pictures do not necessarily need to be very professional. The key thing is having the pictures highlight the main features and functions of the goods you are promoting. The pictures should appeal vast audience on Instagram.

Videos too are important in Instagram marketing. You can create and share a video with your employees to promote the product at hand.

You can also opt to do a live product review video and share it on Instagram. Pictures and videos are more appealing to many people than text files. Media files stand higher chances of going viral as people share them. They are also more memorable than text files. Create photos and videos that show your brand story and values. So images and videos are important if you want to improve your brand and sales.

2. Use quality media

To improve your visibility, you need to make and share high-quality photos and videos in your feeds. Where necessary, seek professional assistance or advice from a photographer. However, you can use a great camera to take sharp pictures. Try to get your images at best angles. Edit your photos for better results. Nowadays mobile phones are equipped with photo editing tools for this purpose. Instagram too has several photo editing tools. Apply these tools for your Instagram marketing purpose.

3. Connect with our followers

Maintaining contact with your customers is vital, particularly for developing business with a small market share. You can start by showing your clients that you are concerned about their feedback. You can achieve this by replying to their questions and comments.

This will improve user-generated content and credibility as well as promote the visibility of your products and business. Your Instagram followers can significantly influence the success of your enterprise, and you should never underestimate them.

4. Use hashtags

Hashtags are relevant in Instagram marketing. You need to use them because Instagram users interact using hashtags. Hashtags allow users to make your contents searchable and are important if you want to increase your followers. Hashtags like media can create a viral effect which is beneficial to your business. You can also take advantage of trending hashtags especially if the hashtags are related to your product. This is important because Instagram users can use hashtags to search for posts.

5. Use branded hashtag

You should include your business name in your hashtags. Use unique hashtags for a particular promotional campaign you run. Not only does this promote your campaign, but it also provides a unique hashtag for your clients to connect and share with other participants.

6. Have a friendly attitude to everyone

While carrying out your Instagram marketing, you need to understand that Instagram is a community composed of people with varied ideas, emotions, and background. Always be friendly to everyone and appreciate their time to connect with you on your page. Always ensure you listen to your clients.

7. Be active

Post at least once daily to keep things up to date and ensure your followers updated with the current happenings. You can experiment posting at varying times of the day to see which time your posts do best.

8. Consistency

Consistency is crucial in Instagram marketing. Be consistent in your postings and develop a theme that is prominent in your posts. Let your followers know what to expect from you.

9. Link your Instagram and Facebook accounts

Connect your Instagram and Facebook accounts to improve your marketing power. Nowadays, you can have an Instagram tab on your Facebook page. This allows you to share your Instagram posts to your Facebook followers if you have a fan page.

You can network with friends and the world via Instagram. Instagram can be used for marketing purposes. Instagram marketing can improve your brand's visibility, increase sales, and consequently revenues. Consider the above mentioned Instagram marketing tips to achieve success.

INSTAGRAM MARKETING STRATEGY

As a business owner always on the lookout for new ways to market your products and services, you'd want to consider Instagram for your social media marketing plan. As one of the world's fastest-growing social networks, Instagram has over 800 million active users' worldwide, generating 40 million images per day. If these figures don't impress you, we don't know what else would! Needless to say, this image-based social network provides countless of possibilities for brand marketing. Use this site to engage and influence existing and potential customers. Below, you'll find some tips on how to market with Instagram.

1. Post authentic content. This is a no-brainer tip that many still fail to follow. Content should always be real, about real people and things. Imaginary and made-up stuff have no room in any social media site. These would discredit you and negatively affect your business image.

2. Share high quality content. What defines high quality? Posts that are not only attractive but also interesting, informative, and engaging can be described as such. Also, you'd want to post something that would be of great help to your audience. Post a step-by-step photo on how to refurbish an old piece of wooden furniture if your business is a home improvement shop.

3. Be consistent. The problem with some business owners is that they don't have the time to post as often as necessary. Or some are just too lazy to do that. Whatever is the reason behind your inconsistency, you should do something about it. Maximize Instagram's marketing prowess by being consistent with the frequency of your posts. If business keeps you away from the computer during most of the day, consider hiring a social media specialist to do these things for you.

4. Use relevant hashtags. Hashtags help make your posts more visible to your audience. Be sure to use a lot of it, but choose those that are highly relevant to your business, and are suitable to the context of your posts.

5. Build relationships. As with other social networks, Instagram is also a great place for connecting with other people, particularly potential customers. Seek to cultivate relationships with them.

Converse with other users and thank them for sharing images related to your brand.

6. Give the right response to negative feedback. Not all images associated with your brand are positive. Some would be sharing negative images. Don't seek out a war against these users. Instead, take time to reach out to them and find out what's causing the hostility. Address their concern and issues, and thank them for helping you build a better brand. Your professionalism would surely go a long way beyond being admired.

Surely, there are lots of wonderful opportunities for marketing on Instagram. Just make sure that you're on the right track so you can maximize its potential fully.

MARKETING STRATEGY

Posting at the right time

Timing is everything when using Instagram marketing. Your engagement depends on your timing. If you post at a bad time you might end up being unnoticed. Early morning or late in the evening is the optimal time to post. Do not post during or between the 9-5 business hours. The worst day for engagement in a week is Sunday while Monday and Thursday tend to have the highest Instagram follower engagement and traffic.

Follow similar instagram profiles

Follow people who follow the same interest you like. If you follow people with similar interests you will be sure to get noticed. Plus, they are more likely to follow you back. Reach out to people who you believe would be interested in your products.

Get a suitable instagram name

It is unlikely that people will be searching for you by your name unless you are a celebrity. So create names revolving around your business website or the industry that you are working in. Now, when people related to your industry search the relative keywords, it is more likely that your profile will show up. This is a powerful Instagram marketing strategy. Make your "username" identical to what you are selling because that is what people are searching for.

Wisely use the description

When writing your description make sure to let people know about the benefits of you and your business. Add a link to your channel or advertising campaign to direct the people to your page.

Add texts to images and use hashtags

Honestly, Instagram is more about images than plaintexts. Adding images is a great way to let people know how wonderful your product or service is. Use visually strong content that will attract attention.

Everybody needs to use hashtags on Instagram and if you want your business to be noticed then you have use hashtags. Using hashtags will make sure you end up on the list of the trending keywords that people are searching for.

If you want to use Instagram as a marketing channel then you need to use the simple features of Instagram in the most efficient manner. Your Instagram marketing will be a success if you post unique pictures. Also, now you have the 'Instagram stories' feature which is a cool powerful tool that you can use to your advantage. These marketing tips will make you stand out from the rest of the pack. All of the techniques above are an Instagram marketing strategy that will help build a huge fan base.

STEPS FOR EFFECTIVE INSTAGRAM MARKETING

Instagram is increasing in popularity among brands as a powerful social marketing tool. People today enjoy being visually stimulated, which makes a social network that is solely based on image sharing so effective.

When you use social media to share images that relate to your business, you will forge stronger relationships with your current fans and customers plus broaden your reach to find new ones. Not only can you share pictures of your products and the people who work hard to keep your business running (even if it's just you and your pet ferret!), but you can encourage your customers to submit their own pictures of your products being put to use.

It is easy to lose track of time when you log in to your social media accounts. This is especially true with Instagram, where you can easily lose an hour just scanning through the wide variety of images in your stream.

Spending time online is important for your business, but if it's not productive time, then it is simply time wasted. Wasted time does not help bring in new sales. This is why you need to have daily goals for each of your social network activity like when you log on to Instagram.

Before you start your day, know how much time you want to allot to social media and each individual network. Stick with that time limit so that you can be sure you are getting the most important tasks done in your time frame and don't allow yourself to get sucked into the rabbit hole that is the Internet.

Each time you log on to Instagram, make sure you are doing these three things to maintain a high level of efficiency to grow your brand presence:

Add to the number of people you follow

Give yourself about 10-15 minutes each day to start looking for Instagram users in your target market. You can do this by looking at who is following your competitors. Find people who are more engaging with the brands they follow since they are more likely to engage with you as well. Are they leaving comments and liking photos often?

Since social media is all about give and take, make sure that you are following a good number of other people and businesses and bloggers. Do your own fair share of liking and commenting as well.

Share your own content

Take 10 minutes a day to add new unique content to your own Instagram account. People want to see that you have a good amount of interesting content for them to look at if they are going to follow you.

If they look at your stream and only see two pictures and nothing new added in the last month or more, they aren't going to see a reason to become a follower.

If you don't have any unique content to share, set up a time each day to simply focus on taking pictures to share. It can be shots of your products, your office, employees, etc. If it relates to your brand and business, take an interesting shot of it and edit it to your liking and share.

Be interactive

It's no surprise that when you have a social media account, people expect you to be, well, social. Don't simply sign up for an account and then wait for people to start following you.

To be successful in your Instagram marketing, you need to be actively engaging. Reply to comments left on your images, even if it's a simple thank you. Ask questions and encourage a dialog with your followers.

Visit your followers' streams and those of the people that you are following and like images and leave comments. Showing that you will be interactive with other users will go a long way in building your own brand's following.

Instagram will be around for a long time. To be the most effective, you need to be ready to spend time with your account and be productive with that time.

Is your business using Instagram to market your brand? How is it going?

PHOTO TIPS TO BOOST YOUR INSTAGRAM MARKETING

Instagram has 52 times greater engagement level than Facebook and 127 times greater than Twitter. What this means is there's a substantial opportunity for businesses to market a wide range of products and services on Instagram to get maximum sales and profits.

Your Instagram page is a way to make a great first impression on any potential prospects. And the best way to make an awesome first impression is to take great photos and videos.

1. Lighting

Bear in mind that no amount of filtering or editing will save a photo that's badly lit. Use natural light whenever you can, except in cases where you have access to the right kind of lighting set-up. If you're taking pictures outside, early morning and late afternoon are the best times.

2. Use your eyes

Before you take out your phone and start snapping pictures, take a moment to really look at what's going on around you. Use your eyes to structure the photo in your mind. Don't just take out your smartphone and start snapping.

What's in the background of the photo? Is someone about to walk in front of your subject? Is there something going on nearby that might mean taking this picture in a different location would be a better idea? Spend some time looking at your subject, your surroundings, lighting and everything else that is going on before you start clicking away.

3. Use technology

Instagram provides a variety of filters and editing tools. There are also third-party apps which improve the capability of your smartphone camera. There's nothing improper with using apps and tools to take good pictures. Most smartphones have some kind of photo adjusting features and built into their cameras.

They usually include tools that let you cut, switch, modify lighting and contrast levels, increase or decrease saturation, add shadows, shades and highlights and create the long exposure effects.

4. Move around your subject

The lens of smartphone camera soaks up light in a different way in comparison to a traditional camera. When looking through your phone at your subject while moving through a full circle, you'll see how the shifting direction of your light sources can uncover some fantastic effects and surprising results. You'll start to observe opportunities that previously didn't occur when you just held your phone up and clicked a picture.

5. Change your viewpoint

Shooting from up high or right down on the ground can result in more interesting pictures and makes your theme look different. Photos that stand out get shared. This is how a single photograph on Instagram can go viral, earn you hundreds or even thousands of followers, and help you draw attention to your business.

Chapter 7: Growing Your Profile And Audience

When you first get started on Instagram, you may have a few followers. You may have some people who come from your email list, some followers from your other accounts, and some who just randomly find you when they are searching around the platform. But the truth is, your following in the beginning is going to be pretty small. Many people may not even know you are there. But if you want to extend your reach and get the most out of this platform, then you will need to spend your time learning how to grow your profile and get a larger audience or a larger following.

The good news is there are a lot of different ways that you can grow your audience and therefore your business with the help of Instagram. Let's take some time to look at some of the best secrets and tips that you can follow in order to get more followers to your business page.

Like and comment on posts in your niche

In one online conference, the CEO of Freshly Picked, Susan Petersen, spent some time talking about how she was able to take her Instagram account and grow it to 400,000 followers at the time (since then she has expanded her following to 800,000). Petersen states that when she was first getting started, she would spend hours each night looking through pictures on Instagram and liking them.

While this may seem like it takes a lot of work, it has worked for many other Instagram marketers in the past. Her advice for businesses and individuals who are trying to grow their reach is to go through and like about five to ten pictures on someone else's account. It is even better if you are able to go through and leave a genuine comment on the account and even follow that person before you leave.

What this does is gets your name out there so that others are able to discover you. First, the owner of the page is going to see that you spent some time on their page and they will want to return the favor. Then the followers of that page will start to see your name pop up and it may pique their curiosity. They may check out your page and even decide to follow you, growing your reach even more from a few minutes of work.

The best way to do this is to find users that are in your niche. You can do this by checking out hashtags that go with your niche or view the followers of some of your favorite names on Instagram. However, make sure that when you do this, you show some genuine personality, rather than being spammy. People can tell when you are trying to use them or spam them, and they will ignore you in two seconds if they feel like that is what you are doing.

Come up with a theme for the pictures on your page

Write down a few words that you would like people to think about when they come to your page and then use those to help you come up with a theme. This helps to keep the whole page cohesive and looking like it is supposed to go together and can really seem inviting to your followers and any potential followers who are checking out the page.

Spend your time socializing

The more that you can interact, engage with, and socialize with your followers, the better results that you will get. Make sure that you respond to any comments that are left on your page and spend time commenting and liking posts of other influencers in your industry.

When you are commenting, make sure to put some thought and effort behind the words that you say. Don't just leave a comment like "cute!", because this only takes two seconds and the other person will barely notice it. But don't spend time writing three paragraphs about your own business either, because this will come off as being really spammy. Leave comments that are genuine, ask questions, and encourage others to interact back with you.

Create your own hashtag and get others to use this too

This is a great way to help out your business because it can ensure that you gain a lot of new content for your own account, and it can build up a community that will really benefit you in the future. The first thing that you need to do here is to create a hashtag that is unique. Double check to see if it is already being used or not. You want to go with something that is unique, easy to remember, and hopefully relates back to your business in some way or another.

Once you have the hashtag created, you can ask your followers to use it. This is going to be successful if you have a specific purpose for the tag. For example, the company known as A Beautiful Mess will encourage their followers to use the hashtag #ABMLifeIsolorful on all of their happy and colorful pictures.

After some of your followers have started to use this hashtag (and make sure that you are using it as well), you can then repost these images from the followers.

Make sure that you give the follower credit for the picture, but this provides you with a lot of fresh content that you don't even have to think up. Not only is this method able to build up some community in your industry because you show your followers that you really appreciate their pictures, but it ensures that you get fresh content for your own account.

Try out a contest

Another thing that you may want to try out is running a contest. If you have a product that you can give away or something that you are willing to give away to help grow your business, then it may be a good idea for you to run a contest. There has to be a catch though. For example, for someone to have a chance of winning the contest, users need to repost a specific image and then tag you in the caption. Or you can invite your followers to use a special hashtag that you design and then use it on their own images.

If you feel like really expanding this out and getting other Instagram names on board, you can consider doing a giveaway. You can get on board with a few other profiles and influencers, and then everyone can be a part of this. This helps to give each profile or business a chance to reach new customers and can be a great way to build up your business like never before.

Don't forget those Instagram stories

We already spent some time talking about Instagram stories and all the cool things that you can do with them. But make sure that you actually take the time to use a few of these. You don't necessarily need to do one of these each day, but doing one each week or every few days, can really help you connect with your customers and your followers.

These short clips may not seem like much, but since most of your followers are going to be visual, they can make a big difference. Plus, these videos are more interactive and engaging than traditional posts, so they can help you there as well. Having a good mixture of good posts and stories can help that customer base grow faster than ever before.

Encourage your followers to take some actions

It may seem pretty simple, but you will find that your followers are more likely to do something if you actually ask them to do it, rather than just assuming they are going to do it for you. Are you sharing a quote with your followers? Then ask them to like the post if they happen to agree with it. Are you sharing something that is considered relatable or funny? Then ask your followers to tag some of their friends or share the post. Ask your followers some open-ended questions, have them share information about a contest, and find other ways to get the customer engaged as much as possible.

The reason that you do this is to promote some more engagement with the stories that you are doing. The more engagement you get, the higher your account will show up, and the easier it is for new and interested followers to find you. Always ask your followers to show some interest in your posts and you will be amazed at how much more they are willing to participate.

Add a geotag to your pictures

Another tip that you will want to try out is adding a geotag on your picture. There are a lot of different ways that you are able to do this and you are likely to find a lot of success when it comes to this. For example, if you just took a picture of a really cool new restaurant or a city that you traveled to, and then you decide to use that as one of your postings on Instagram, then take the time to geotag it.

When you add a geotag to your account, other people who used that same kind of tagging are able to see that picture as well. When they see that connection, they may be more willing to follow you because they already noticed that you both have something in common. It may seem like such a little thing, but that small connection is often enough to get people to start following your account. It is a simple thing to do and only takes you a few seconds, but you will be surprised at how many followers you can get with this method.

Learn what your followers actually like

It isn't going to do you any good to work on a bunch of posts if the things you post are turning your customers off. Remember, your customers have complete control over whether they are going to check you out or not. You must make sure that you are posting things that your customer actually likes. This encourages the followers to stay, gets them to share the information with others, and can get your followers to engage better.

To figure out what things your customers like the most, it is time to do some research. Go through all of those posts and pictures that you have on your profile and check out which ones ended up with the most comments and likes. You can also check out which ones had the least comments and like. This helps you to see what seems to click with your audience and then tailor your message and your future posts to that.

Link Instagram to some of the other social media sites you are on.

As a business owner, you probably have other social media platforms that you are going to be on. If you are on Facebook, Twitter, or even have a blog, then you may make the assumption that all of your followers are already following you on each of these platforms. But in reality, they are probably only following you on just one of these platforms.

To help increase the number of followers you have, make sure to send out a quick message on the other platforms you are on to let your followers know they can now follow you on Instagram. You may be surprised at how many followers you are able to get this way.

Approach other users that are popular in your niche and set up a collaboration

111

This is an idea that will ask you to think outside the box a little bit. Take some time to research a few of the other profiles in your niche and then talk to them about doing a collaboration. For this, you can ask them to talk you up or ask if you can take over their account as a guest contributor. You will find that doing an Instagram story takeover can be a lot of fun and can even grow your following in the process. In return, you let that influencer do the same on your page.

What this does is introduces both parties to brand new audiences, audiences that they may have never had a chance to meet without this opportunity. Both of you can benefit as followers hear the stories, learn about the other person, and decide to start following you. The more times you are able to do this, the bigger you can grow your audience.

As you get used to working with Instagram, you will find that the most important thing you can do is grow your audience. The more followers you are able to get to your page, the more potential customers you get to work with. Using some of the tips and secrets that we have above, you will be able to get more followers to your account in no time.

The Logo

You might have probably written and implemented a social media marketing campaign for your brand but don't have a logo design, yet. A logo is quintessential for your brand and it is critical for any marketing strategy. If your brand has a logo, then people will forever associate your business with that logo whenever they see it. A logo is an important part of branding, especially when you want to make the most of social media and market your business online.

A logo is a part of a brand's identity and it helps potential and existing customers recognize your brand. It also gives brand recognition to your target audience. Whenever someone sees your logo online, it is only natural that they will be curious to learn more about your business and what you do.

So, where does your logo come into the picture in terms of social media marketing? A logo might be small, but it is an important component that contributes to the success of a social media campaign.

As a marketer, it is critical that your existing and potential customers see your brand logo daily. You can embed it on your photos, maybe in one corner; you can add it as a watermark on posts on any of your social media platforms or even use it as your Instagram profile picture. In this manner, your customers will form a perception of your brand that will stay with them forever. The logo plays a very important part in your social media marketing campaign in the following ways.

Promotes Your Business

How can you identify a business without reading anything about it? You can recognize it from its logo. Doesn't a big, bright M remind you of delicious burgers?

People might wonder how a logo may sell a business out in public.

A logo is an important image with the ability of sticking in the minds of the viewers. Usually, a good and well-structured logo design can promote your business by itself.

A logo conveys a lot and also acts as an introduction to others. You don't have to say much once someone sees your business logo. A good logo says a lot about what you stand for and what you offer, without necessarily uttering any words. For instance, you don't need to be told what that simple tick-like logo on your shoes, training gear or your cap means, do you? The logo tells you about the brand, doesn't it?

Creates an Identity

At times, content isn't sufficient to get the word out there. All the content you post will not make any sense if your brand doesn't have a sense of identity.

A logo helps create an identity for your brand.

In fact, without a logo, you will also end up like a lot of the other startup marketers on the web who create and post a lot of content in the hopes of generating traffic to their website. This approach might produce some results. Nonetheless, your logo will greatly communicate who you are and what your business is all about.

In many instances, a logo tends to attract people so much that they are curious enough to want to know more about your products and services.

Shows Professionalism

As a marketer, you need to maintain a certain degree of professionalism. You can display professionalism by doing something as simple as including a logo on every Instagram marketing post you make.

It will make your customers feel comfortable while doing business with you. Additionally, if you have a high-quality and interesting logo, it will make your content and your brand stand out among your competition.

With time, you will realize that a logo might be sufficient to get the audience to want to build a relationship with you. If they like your logo, they will like your creativity and the way you communicate.

For instance, people love the logo of Apple and in fact, they don't mind spending huge sums of money to acquire Apple products to flaunt the logo.

Who and What You Are

When you start to post and share content on Instagram, it is important to place your logo on your content with the URL of your website.

In turn, your followers will start visiting your website often. This is when you can start to reap the benefits of the content you share. Therefore, start to believe in your credibility. Know that when people trust your credibility and expertise, they will want to be involved with you and your brand.

In Instagram marketing, this is the ultimate objective of any marketer.

A logo does provide a lot of benefits, but there are a couple of things that you must keep in mind before you select a specific logo. You need to carry out an extensive research before you create your logo. Typically, the logo must be perfectly in sync with your brand and theme colors. You need to understand that your logo and your brand will ultimately mean the same thing to the customers.

Select an effective logo name: it needs to be unique and memorable. If your logo involves abbreviations/letters, ensure that it easily rolls off everyone's tongue. It needs to be easy to understand and simple to pronounce.

The logo needs to be pleasing to the eye of the viewer. You need to make it simple and easy to identify with.

In case you are not sure whether your logo will be effective and powerful or not, gather information through focus groups. The easiest way to do this is to create a group and invite people whose opinions you value. Take a little while to evaluate their feedback and then you can create a logo.

Create the Perfect Logo

There are a lot of aspects that you need to consider when you design a logo and they include the font you use, the tagline, designs, colors and more.

When you are designing a logo for social media, there are a couple of different variables that you need to keep in mind. Also, even if you create a perfect logo, your work doesn't end there.

Creating a good logo is one of the steps of online marketing and your work as a marketer has only just begun. In this section, you will learn about certain tips that will help create a logo that will give you an attractive online presence.

The first thing that you need to consider is the aspect ratio.

You might or might not be able to use your logo as is. A couple of social media sites require you to convert your logo to a square or reduce its measurements to a square-shaped thumbnail. It doesn't mean that your logo needs to be perfectly square, but it must have the flexibility of being easily converted into one. Your logo must be able to fit into a small space, so avoid using a lot of unnecessary space while creating a logo.

Once you select a logo, you need to consistently use the same logo on all social media platforms. An effective social media marketing strategy includes different social networking platforms and your logo will be featured on multiple platforms. Therefore, use the same logo on all platforms. Consistency will impact the way your audience perceives your brand. If they see different logos on different platforms, it will confuse them, and they might not be able to recognize your brand.

While designing the logo, you can use detached text and graphics. You need to make sure that the text and graphics you use are separate components of the logo. This will come in handy when you need to convert your logo into a different size. In fact, a lot of brands and companies tend to use a single letter or a graphic in social media to ease its conversion.

Simplicity matters a lot. Further, it also poses the risk of the logo or some of its elements becoming unrecognizable when you resize the logo.

Keeping this in mind, it is a good idea to avoid long taglines, thin lines and intricately detailed graphics when you design a logo. Try to limit the colors and shades you use. A logo created with two or three colors works better on social media because it stands out and is visible in the crowd. If you think you don't possess the necessary skills to design a logo, you can always hire a graphic designer to help you.

When it comes to the overall success of your marketing campaign on Instagram, your logo is one thing that you cannot ignore. It helps create an identity for your brand. Even if a logo is a small aspect of a social media marketing campaign, it is a vital aspect that you cannot overlook.

Instagram Bio

It is important that you understand the different components that comprise your Instagram bio. Once you do this, you can add more details and improve your account to ensure that the users understand what your brand is all about and what they can expect when they follow you.

The main problem that you face when you compose a bio is the little space you have.

The Instagram section for the bio allows only 150 characters. Your username must fit under 30 characters.

With over 800 million users active on the app, you need to optimize all your chances of being discovered and follow an effective marketing strategy. In this section, you will learn about the different things you need to keep in mind to create a brilliant Instagram bio.

The Profile Picture

Your Instagram profile page needs to include a profile photo relevant to your business or brand. The photo you use can be a logo or it can be a product photo.

Whatever you select as your profile photo, it needs to be attractive and the viewer must be able to easily associate it with your business. Usually a lot of companies, celebrities, brands and influencers use a verified badge on their profile photo to identify themselves.

One feature of Instagram is that it crops the uploaded profile picture into a circle. It means that your profile photo will be visible, and you need to be careful to make sure that it stays clear and visible even after cropping. You don't have to worry about uploading a photo with a square shape featuring your brand photo or logo right at the center. After all, the corners will be cut off without cutting off your branding.

Username and Name

The username and the name are searchable in Instagram's search field. The username appears at the top of your Instagram profile and it will be quite prominent, and it will appear in bold text. Like mentioned earlier, it is important that you carefully select a username and a name.

If you have a simple and a short name, then the search results will show your profile easily. After the search, the name will appear in gray right below the profile's handle.

Public Profile

You need to make sure that your Instagram handle is public and not private.

You will be shooting yourself in the leg if your profile is set as a private account. If your profile is a private account, then all those who visit your profile will not be able to view any of the photos you post.

It will act as an immediate deterrent and will prevent people from following you. To prevent all this, you simply need to make sure that you go to your account's settings and turn off the "Private Account" setting. If you have a business profile on Instagram, by default it will be a public account.

Bio

The bio includes a short description and a synopsis of what you and your business are all about. A lot of companies use this space to list the products or services they offer, their website's URL, their location and their physical address. You need to keep the bio short because you only have 150 characters to convey all that you want to.

Website

In the bio, you can include your website's URL to increase the visibility of your business and it also encourages those who visit your profile to visit the business website for more information. In this field, ensure you add a link to your website and don't skip it. After all, you need a landing page where you can direct all the traffic.

Category

This is a feature that is only available for a business account. This category appears below a company's name and is directly linked to the one selected on the related Facebook page. For instance, indicating that you are in the restaurant business or a public figure is as easy as selecting the appropriate category.

Call-to-Action Buttons

To activate the call-to-action buttons you need to fill out the necessary information that includes your email address, phone number and location. Previously, business account users used to write their email addresses and location address in the bio section.

This feature has been added for business account set up to free up some space in the bio section. Keep in mind that this feature is only shown in the app view and not the web view. You can find this feature by going to the Edit profile option and then select Contact Options.

Email

When you add an email address to the bio, it creates an email button on your profile. Whenever someone clicks on the email option, the app promptly opens their default email app on their device. It makes it easier for your followers and potential customers to communicate with you through email.

Directions

If you want to give your location, this is the field where you need to enter your physical address and help customers locate you easily. When a customer clicks on this button, it will prompt them to the default map application on their device.

Call

Perhaps the best and the most convenient contact information is to add your business phone number. Using a phone call to communicate is the most personal form of communication. Whenever someone clicks on the call button, they will be prompted to use their default call application to make a call.

Recently, Instagram also released a new feature that allows you to use hashtags and profile links in the bio. It opens up a wide range of possibilities for marketers to use hashtags. For instance, if your brand has different Instagram handles for different aspects of your business; you can include a link to your other handles in your bio instead of making your followers search for them. It certainly makes it easier for people to find your handles especially when your accounts are not yet verified.

You can increase your visibility and relevance once you understand the ways in which you can optimally use the different components of your bio. A good bio will make more sense to your followers.

How to Write the Bio

An Instagram bio tells the followers and other Instagrammers about the nature of your business. Essentially, it is a short description of yourself.

To make an impression, the bio needs to be concise and catchy. A catchy bio can lure people into following you and make them want to do business with you. If

Instagram marketing is your main objective, ensure that you come up with a killer bio. Here are a couple of things that you need to keep in mind to create a brilliant bio.

Include a Tagline

If you want to make your bio fascinating, use a tagline. A tagline will tell the viewers what your business is all about in a couple of words. Similarly, you can also use a summary of your company's values or add a mission statement to your bio.

Be Minimalistic

A perfect Instagram bio is always short and simple. You need to provide all that information that your targeted customers will need to recognize the primary objective of your brand. You don't have to fill your bio with a lot of information, just stick to the essential components. After all, a visitor can browse through your Instagram posts or visit your website to find out more about your business.

Link Your Account

It will make your bio efficient and will keep it to the point. You can link your Instagram account with your accounts on Facebook, Twitter, and Snapchat will allow your followers to easily find your company on other social media platforms. It increases your reach and increases your online visibility.

A Branded Hashtag

A branded hashtag allows other Instagram users to share their content for you on their feed. A user can use your hashtag and this improves the scope of interacting with your audience. It also helps create a convincing brand story. If you have a branded hashtag, you need to include it in your bio.

Branded hashtags aren't restricted to just products and you can obtain one even for the services you provide. For instance, service provided could combine an emoji and a branded hashtag to set up a feed

134

that will humanize their brand and make it seem more engaging. You need to remember that the clickable hashtags are only in the Instagram web interface and not on the mobile app.

Use Emojis

Using emojis can really go a long way in helping a user to convey the personality and identity of a brand. Emojis can be used as an alternate for certain words and you can free up some space in your bio. Emojis also make Instagram posts and bio appear more exciting.

Emojis are quite cute and you might want to use them a lot, but it is a good idea to incorporate them in the Instagram bio toolbox. From faces to animals to other symbols, whichever emoji you choose will create a sense of brand personality.

An emoji can be worth a thousand words and will help you tell more about your brand than words can. In fact, you can effectively communicate using emojis and reduce the words you use. It will also help free up some space in your bio. Emojis are nice and have a certain appeal to them, but you need to remember that you must not go overboard with the emoji. Don't fill

136

up your bio with emojis. After all, the viewers are not there to play Pictionary.

Use Line Breaks

Using line breaks in an Instagram bio serves as a clear illustration of your proficiency in Instagram and its features. Even more, it makes a profile look more engaging and consumable.

Include a Call-to-Action

When creating a perfect bio, keep in mind that you cannot avoid a proper call to action. Without a call-to-action, your bio is incomplete. The call to action must drive your targeted audience to visit your online store, access your website, call or email you for more information. Ask yourself what exactly you want visitors to do after viewing your profile before you decide a call-to-action.

Include Contact Information

Providing a contact in your bio is very essential. Just imagine having a follower who is impressed by your business and

137

wants to get in touch with you but does not have the contact.

This requires the need to include your contact information in your bio. It may be a phone number or an email address. Rather than just leaving a comment in the posts, users can reach out to you directly.

What Makes You Unique?

What makes you unique compared to your competitors? State it in your bio and you will see the impact. Notably, customers want to get the best there is in the market and preferably from the most unique seller. When marketing, clearly indicate what makes you the best in your line of work.

A good Instagram profile must accurately describe what the business is about and what it can perfectly deliver. Provide unique skills and services to lure potential clients into not only following you but also to buy and make consecutive purchases from your business.

Include other fun facts about your brand because it is a great way to showcase the company's personality.

Keep all these steps in mind and you can easily create an interesting and engaging Instagram bio in no time. The one thing

you must never forget while creating a bio
is the character limit placed on it.

Chapter 8: How To Connect To A Facebook Catalog

You have a few options to connect a catalog to Instagram. You can create a shop on Facebook, create a catalog in Business Manager, or set up a shop for Facebook in Shopify or BigCommerce.

Create a Shop on Facebook

Adding a shop section to your Facebook Page is a great option, as the process is straightforward. Unfortunately, it's currently only available to users in the U.S.

Step One: On your Page, click the "Shop" tab. If there is no Shop tab at the moment, head to "Settings" and find "Edit Page." Click "Add a Tab" and choose "Shop."

Step Two: Agree to the terms of service (this may involve entering your password) and click "Continue."

Step Three: Choose your currency

Step Four: Then you're ready to start adding products!

Create a Catalog in Business Manager

An option available to everyone is to create a catalog in Business Manager.

Step One: Open your Business Manager account.

Step Two: Head to "People and Assets" in settings.

Step Three: In "Product Catalogs," either select a catalog you already have or click "Add New Product Catalog" and then "Create a New Product Catalog." Give the catalog a name and specify what types of products you will be adding, then click "Create Product Catalog."

Step Four: With your catalog set up, you can add a product feed. Choose a feed name, a currency, and the upload type.

Step Five: Create the product feed and save your file in CSV or TSV format.

Set Up a Shop on Shopify

To add a shop in your Shopify account, click "+" next to "Sales Channel." Choose "Facebook" and click "Add channel."

Now, connect to your Facebook account by heading to "Facebook," then "Account," and finally "Connect Account." Make sure that you pick the same one as is connected to your Instagram business account.

Wait until Facebook approves your store to use the products for shoppable posts on Instagram.

Set Up a Shop on BigCommerce

Before you can set up a shop, your BigCommerce store needs to be launched and accessible. Once you've confirmed that is, go to "Channel Manager" and click on "Get Started."

Review the requirements that appear and click "Get Started."

Complete your shop by providing BigCommerce with your contact information, your Facebook Page, and the URL of your storefront terms of service. Also select your preferred checkout.

Like with Shopify, you'll need to wait for Facebook to review your catalog.

149

HOW TO CREATE SHOPPABLE POSTS

Step One: Connect Your Catalog

Once you've done the above, you'll need to wait a little more time for Instagram to review your catalog. As soon as it's approved, you'll receive a notification in the Instagram app. When you've received the notification, find the Shopping section in settings and click "Products." You can now chose your product catalog and connect it to your business profile.

Step Two: Tag Your Posts

Create a new post that you want to make shoppable. Upload your image and add the captions, effects, and filters just as your normally do. When you reach the tagging stage, you'll have the chance to tag your products. Click "Tag Products," search for the products you want, and select them. Finally, click "Done" — your shoppable post is complete!

That's it!

ADVANCED INSTAGRAM STRATEGIES

This section will explore advanced Instagram marketing strategies not many marketers know about. Very few marketers use Micro Influencers to achieve the kinds of results our campaigns offer because today, Influencer marketing is so focused on Macro Influencers. We already explored the limitations of macro influencers in the "Micro Influencers" section of this course. But now, we will discuss the insane power of Micro Influencers.

STRATEGY ONE:

RANKING CONTENT IN THE HASHTAG SEARCH RESULTS

Utilizing Micro Influencers allows you to achieve economies of scale where they matter most on Instagram... likes and comments.

Marketing is all about getting your product in front of as many "Active Consumers" as possible. Active consumers are people actively searching for your product or service. On Instagram, these "Active Consumers" are using Instagram's search engine to discover products they are interested in. For instance, let's pretend you own a Yoga Apparel brand. Your objective would be to get your "Shoppable Instagram Posts" to rank at the top of the Hashtag search results for #YogaPants, #Yoga, #YogaApparel and so on.

With over 250,000 unique impressions an hour for just the Hashtag #YogaPants, getting a shoppable post to rank at the top of the search results would result in a tremendous amount of exposure and product sales.

When you consider each Instagram post should contain 15-25 Hashtags, getting one post to rank at the top of the search results page would amount to millions of impressions per hour. In addition to sales, your posts will also generate thousands of new followers you can remarket to.

HASHTAG SEARCH RESULT RANKING FACTORS

There are several factors that Instagram takes into account when ranking content in the Hashtag search results. Understanding these factors will help you see how vital Micro Influencers are in overcoming these ranking barriers.

Number and Frequency of Likes - This is the most important factor in determining what posts rise to the top of the search results. The number of likes is important, but equally important is how quickly likes are obtained after the post is added to your feed. This is where Micro Influencers offer tremendous value. Remember how we suggested setting up content drips that then trigger an email and text message alerting the Influencer to your new content. This will allow you to generate hundreds of "Likes" in a short amount of time.

In order to rank at the top of your industry hashtags, you can do a little research and see how many "Likes" the top ranked posts currently have in relation to how long ago they were posted. This will also help you determine how many Influencers you need to engage for your campaign in order to overcome these ranking barriers and benefit from this strategy.

Percentage of Comments in relation to the number of likes - There is a ranking correlation between the number of "Likes"

154

and the number of "Comments" each post receives. Posts with lots of likes but a disproportionate number of comments won't rank as high.

User Authority - Instagram ranks users according to the level of engagement they receive over all their posts. If you have lots of followers but low levels of engagement in terms of likes and comments, your User Authority will suffer. Accounts with lots of fake followers will drive down your user authority so never purchase fake followers. Running a Micro Influencer campaign will drive up your "User Authority" tremendously. As Micro Influencers engage with your brand on Instagram, a higher percentage of your "Followers" will like and comment on your posts. This will make it easier for you to rank in the Hashtag search results.

Content Type - Instagram ranks video content higher than image based content. Thus, having video content mixed with "Shoppable Instagram Posts" is recommended to maximize the amount of content that gets ranked.

Chapter 9: 6 Smart Ways To Make Money Online With Your Instagram Page

One of the neat things about Instagram is that there are a lot of different ways that you can earn money through this platform. While this guidebook has spent a lot of time talking about how businesses can grow their following and earn customers, the same tips can be used for individuals who are looking to earn money online.

A business may decide to just sell their own products online to customers and make a profit that way, but there are other methods that small businesses (depending on who they are) and individuals can use to earn a very nice income online from all the hard work they have done to gain followers and a good reputation on this platform. Let's take a look at some of the different ways that you can potentially make money on Instagram.

Way #1 – Affiliate Marketing

Affiliate Marketing

The first option is to work as an affiliate marketer. Basically, with this option, you are going to promote a product for a company and then get paid for each sale. This is something that is really popular with bloggers because they work on getting their website set up, and then they can write articles about a product, or sell advertising space, and then they make money on any sales through their links. You can do the same thing with Instagram as well.

When you want to work with affiliate marketing with Instagram, you need to post attractive images of the products you choose and try to drive sales through the affiliate URL. You will get this affiliate link through the company you choose to advertise with. Just make sure that you are going with an affiliate that offers high-quality products so you don't send your followers substandard products. And check that you will actually earn a decent commission on each one.

Once you get your affiliate URL, add it to the captions of the posts you are promoting or even in the bio if you plan to stick with this affiliate for some time. It is also possible for you to hook up the Instagram profile and blog so that when people decide to purchase through the link at all, you will get the sale.

If you have a good following on Instagram already, then this method of making money can be pretty easy. You just need to find a product that goes with the theme of your page and then advertise it to your customers. Make sure that the product is high-quality so that your customers are happy with the recommendations that you give.

Way #2

Create Sponsored Post

Instagram users that have a following that is pretty engaged have the ability to earn some money through the platform simply by creating sponsored content that is original and that various brands can use. To keep it simple, a piece of sponsored product through Instagram could be a video or a picture that is going to highlight a brand or a specific product. These posts are then going to have captions that include links, @mentions, and branded hashtags.

While most brands don't really need a formal brand ambassadorship for the creators of this kind of content, it is pretty common for some of these brands to find certain influencers to help them come up with new content over and over again. However, you must make sure that the brands and the products that you use are a good fit for the image that you worked so hard to create on Instagram. You want to showcase some brands that you personally love and can get behind. Then you can show the followers that you have how this brand is already fitting into your lifestyle so they can implement it as well.

Way #3

Sell Pictures

This one is one that may seem obvious, but it can be a great way for photographers to showcase some of the work that you do. If you are an amateur or professional photographer, you will find that Instagram is the perfect way to advertise and even sell your shots. You can choose to sell your services to big agencies or even to individuals who may need the pictures for their websites or other needs.

If you are posting some of the pictures that you want to sell on your profile, make sure that each of them has a watermark on them. This makes it hard for customers to take the pictures without paying you first. You can also use captions to help list out the details of selling those pictures so there isn't any confusion coming up with it at all.

To make this one work, take the time to keep your presence on Instagram active. This ensures that the right people and the right accounts are following. This is also a good place to put in the right hashtags so that people are able to find your shots. You may even want to take the time to get some engagement and conversations started with big agencies in the photography world who can help you grow even more.

Way #4

Promote Your Services, Products, or Business

If you already run a business, then Instagram can be a good way to market and promote your business. For example, if you already sell some products, use Instagram to post shots of the products, ones that the customer can't already find on your website. Some other ways that you can promote your business through Instagram include:

Behind the scenes: These are very popular on Instagram. Show your followers what it takes to make the products you sell. Show them some of your employees working. Show something that the follower usually won't be able to see because it is unique and makes them feel like they are part of your inner circle.

Pictures from your customers: If you pick out a good hashtag and share it with your customers, they will start to use it with some of their own pictures. You can then use this content to help promote your business even more.

Exclusive offers and infographics: You can take the time to market your services through Instagram with some exclusive offers and infographics of your products. This works really well if the offers are ones the customer wouldn't be able to find anywhere else.

Way #5

Sell Advertising Space on Your Page

If you have a large enough following, you may be able to get other brands and companies interested in buying advertising on your profile. They will use this as a way to gain access to your followers in order to increase their own followers, sell a product, or increase their own brand awareness. This is the perfect opportunity for you to make some money from all the hard work that you have done for your own page.

There are many different ways that you can do this. You can offer to let them do a video and then post it as your story, promote a post on your profile, or use any other ad options. You can then charge for the type of space they decide to use, the amount of time they want to advertise for, and how big of an audience you are promoting them in front of.

Way #6

Become a Brand Ambassador

This is something that is becoming really popular with MLM companies. There is so much competition on Twitter and Facebook that many are turning to use Instagram as a new way to promote their products and get followers that they may not be able to find through other means. And because of the visual aspects of the platform, these ambassadors can really showcase some of the products through pictures and videos.

There are many companies that you can choose from when it comes to being a brand ambassador. Since you have already taken some time to build up your audience and you have a good following, so if you can find a good product to advertise to your followers, you can make a good amount of money. You have to pick out a product that your followers will enjoy, ones that go with the theme of your profile to enhance your potential profits.

s

Chapter 10: How To Use Paid Advertising On Instagram

Everything we've discussed up until this point has been free advertising. Of course, it's not entirely free as it will take up your time and time is money... but you don't have to pay anybody to make it happen.

Instagram, however, does also offer paid advertising. You may be wondering why you'd want to shell out for Instagram advertisements; after all, even if you stick with the free options, the engagement on Instagram blows nearly any other social media marketing platform out of the water.

The big thing is clickable links. The major problem that many brands run into with advertising on Instagram is that the only clickable link you can post is in your bio, and you need to modify this link every time you have a new promotion or anything you'd want potential customers to engage with. Plus, people actually have to go on your Instagram page to see it, and since many people are simply flipping through their feeds this can be an issue.

Paid Instagram ads solve this problem. With a paid Instagram ad, you can have a "shop now" link or whatever else you'd like in the ad.

In order to post your own Instagram ad... you first need to have a Facebook page, since all Instagram ads are posted through Facebook. So if you are interested in Instagram advertising, you're going to need to setup a Facebook business page first. (Fortunately, this is also free.)

Once you have the Facebook page set up, you'll find that you have a lot of control over how your paid ads get displayed; you can scale how much you want to pay, get comprehensive reporting, and also control what audiences you target (location, age, gender, income, etc.).

There are four different kinds of Instagram paid ads that you can choose from:

•Video: you can post up to 60 seconds of video in either square or landscape shape;

•Carousel: you can post up to 4 photos that people can "swipe" through;

•Photo: you can post one photo in the standard square form;

•Stories: you can use video or photo footage to advertise on Instagram stories.

If you would like to post an ad to Instagram, here is how you do it:

1.Link your Facebook page to your Instagram page. When you are in your Facebook page, choose "Settings" and then "Instagram Ads." Click "Add an Account" and put your Instagram login here. Click "confirm."

2.Create your advertising campaign. Go to "Ads Manager." Click "+ Create Campaign." Here, you can choose the "point" of your campaign - you will have options like "brand awareness" or "engagement" or "traffic" or "conversions" or several more. Choose the one most appropriate for your needs. If you specifically want sales, "conversions" is the most conventional choice.

3.Make your ad. Once you choose the purpose of your campaign, you will be sent to the "Ad Set" page where you can further refine your focus. Once you do this, you can define your target audience (remember, you did this with your "ideal customer" brainstorm!) and then decide how much money that you want to spend on your ad. Then you can select the placement of your ad in Instagram, such as whether you want the ad to appear in Stories, Feed, or the Audience Network. This is also where you decide how much that you want to spend... it's generally a good idea to start low. If your ad is really taking off... spend more, of course! After, you can choose the format of your ad (whether you want a single video or an

170

image or a carousel). Once your visuals are uploaded, on the left side of the screen you will see a place to put your text. Don't forget hashtags! On the right, you'll see a preview of how your ad will appear when it is uploaded to Instagram.

4.Send your ad to Instagram! All you have to do now is hit "finish" and... your ad has been launched!

While the process may sound a little daunting (and a bit strange that you need to set up an Instagram ad in Facebook), once you get the process down it's actually pretty simple.

Again, the major perk of the paid ad is that you get to insert a clickable link. Instagram is magic when it comes to getting engagement... so imagine how much attention that link is going to get!

Chapter 11: Tools, Links And Resources On How To Win With Instagram

Instagram tools are becoming a huge hit online, and it seems like more and more tools are being rolled out all the time. Instagram has a variety of tools, all of which serve a different purpose, but each just as useful as the next at helping you put your best marketing efforts forward. The social media world is a competitive one, and Instagram has proved itself to be a strong contender, continuously coming up with more ways and tools to improve and adapt to the ever-changing world of marketing and advertising. Let's take a look at some of the various tools available and what they're used for.

Best Instagram Scheduling Tools

Here's a list of some of the best tools which can be used for scheduling content on Instagram:

Buffer

In terms of managing social network accounts, Buffer is an absolute timesaver. It allows you to schedule and publish posts on many online platforms like Twitter, Pinterest, and Facebook. It also provides thorough analytics for your online campaigns. Buffer is also available on Instagram. So it gives business owners the flexibility of scheduling posts on Instagram.

Buffer's simplicity in terms of usage is perhaps the most significant thing about it. So, users need not worry about a learning curve or following tutorials. Using Buffer is as simple as these three steps: hooking up your business accounts, scheduling your content, and you are all set.

Buffer allows you to schedule up to a maximum of 10 posts for free, after which you're asked to upgrade to any of their plans for more posting options. Their plans are budget-friendly and go as low as $10 per month. This plan covers up to 10 social media profiles and a hundred scheduled posts.

This one is perfect for scheduling content, and it comes with both a free and pro version (which is paid for). This tool allows users to schedule single-image posts right from their desktops or mobile apps, conveniently allowing you to schedule ahead of time.

Sendible

Sendible can be used to schedule posts, create reports on analytics, collaborate with your entire team, or even reply to the comments of your followers using a social network inbox. It works great for agencies too. You can also use Sendible to make your motivational quote or Instagram image utilizing their canvas integration.

Your videos can also be published directly to your Instagram account from Sendible. The app provides different packages, but their micro package allows up to four social network accounts at $24 per month. They bill annually.

Hootsuite

Hootsuite is a very recognized platform for social media management. You can integrate it with all the core social networks apart from Instagram. With this application, you can automate posts and send reminders for posts. It is not as expensive as the competition, and you can use it as an iOS, Android, or web application.

Even if you develop the best content, posting it at the wrong time may not get you the traffic you want. You need to learn the right posting time for your content. We will be probing this more in the chapter to follow.

Hooper

A great tool for helping you schedule and manage your statistics. This tool is exclusively for Instagram scheduling only, and besides the convenience of scheduling, users can get phone previews to see how their post looks on a mobile device before approving it, content calendars, and even a space for you to save your draft content if there are posts which you want to come back later on and tweak.

Later

The name is a dead giveaway with this one. Later is a scheduling tool, and according to eCommerce Facebook group members, it is one of the most popular Instagram scheduling tools out there. The most notable thing about this tool is its easy scheduler and visual calendar. On top of that, it comes with a link.bio feature, which turns your bio links into -voila! - shoppable URLs. Just what the doctor ordered to peak those sales numbers. Later is a robust post-scheduling Instagram tool. According to the website, they are the go-to company for over 600,000 top brands, influencers, and agencies. It is indeed one of the most popular scheduling tools in the world, serving many entrepreneurs, small companies, and bloggers.

Later also allows you to manage comments on your Instagram. It offers a free plan and a premium plan. On the free plan, users are allowed to schedule not more than 30 posts (only photo posts) per month for a single social profile. Going up to $49 per month from $9 per month, the paid plans support up to a maximum of 5 profiles and unlimited posts.

Schedugram

This tool is perfect for scheduling all types of posts, although it is one of the pricier tools compared to a lot of the other ones mentioned. Schedugram comes with features which include content creation, a feature which is explicitly designed for Instagram. Its built-in photo editing, location, shopping, drag and drop calendar function, mention, carousel ad options, videos, and stories are only a peek into what this tool is capable of.

Tools for Content Creation on Instagram

Here's a list of some of the tools you might find useful for your content creation efforts:

Boomerang

If you love those quirky, funny, short video loops you've become so accustomed to on Instagram, Boomerang is how it's done. It is now a built-in part of Instagram's story features, and it is absolutely perfect for creating on-the-go short video loops anytime, anywhere.

Canva

This tool comes with both free and paid templates for you to choose from to help you create your best content yet. From email headers to Instagram posts, Canva will leave you spoilt for choice when it comes to which templates to use for your

Instagram profile. You can even choose to upload your finished products directly onto your Instagram account once you're happy with it.

Kapwing

If videos and memes are your choices of entertainment, this is the tool you're going to want to use to create them. Specializing in video editing and creation, this free online content-creation tool lets you create memes quickly and efficiently, add music to your texts, resize and trim your videos, create slow-motion content, add subtitles, and more. You'll enjoy browsing through its many features.

PicFlow

This tool is provided free, although it comes with in-app purchases if you need more advanced features at your disposal. PicFlow is a good choice when it comes to turning your photos into a video slideshow, and you can even add on some music to make it a little bit more interesting. PicFlow does come with a watermark though, and you're going to have to pay to get upgraded to have those watermarks removed.

Repost

 For sharing and curating content, Repost is going to be your go-to. With this tool, your favorite videos and photos on Instagram can quickly and easily be reposted (don't forget to give credit to the original owner of the content though if you're reposting anything from a follower or influencer). Reposting can be a big help to your marketing efforts, especially when it comes to encouraging user-generated content. Plus, it's free!

VSCO

A tool that's used for editing your videos and your photos. This one is ideal for all those marketers looking to create some really striking content and visuals for their profiles. VSCO has some pretty powerful video and image-editing features, and when done right, your visuals can look almost as though they were shot professionally. For the more serious content creators, there are preset options available which can be used with other tools like Photoshop and Lightroom.

Tools for Managing Multiple Channels

Managing multiple social media platforms can be challenging and time-consuming, which is why these multi-channel tools can come in handy during these moments:

CrowdFire

With both free and paid options available, this social media account management tool is perfect for the busy marketer who's got a lot on their plate. Run on a web-based platform, this "everything under one roof" social media management tool lets you control your blog content, schedule, publish, curate, and even track your social media mentions all through this one, seamless tool. If you're looking to monitor your post analytics and social media accounts (not just Instagram), CrowdFire can do that for you too.

Sendible

Another multi-channel tool to make life a little more efficient for you is Sendible. The only catch with this one is that it can be a little on the pricier side. This is because it is designed mostly for agencies. Small business owners and those who are just starting out might find the added monthly cost with this one a pinch on the budget, but it does come with some really great, robust features. This tool has got Canva integration, plus team collaborations features, CRM, and account and social media management which make scheduling and managing your Instagram account a breeze if you're willing to spend on it.

Status Rew

A tool that is perfect if you've got 10 social media profiles, 10 Twitter sources, 2000 scheduled posts per profile, and three members running the show. Status Rew has even got social listening features, which generally means you can sync your social engagement to the platform, draft replies, monitor keywords, and even moderate comments without ever having to switch back and forth between Instagram and this tool.

Instagram Influencer Locating Tools

Influencers are everywhere on social media, and sooner or later, you're going to need to work with them, at least once. So why not get on board with some tools that could help you locate the best influencers that your business might consider collaborating with?

UserGems

A tool that is perfect for helping you locate both influencers and even micro-influencers. The best part? These could be among your very own existing customer base! This tool uses real-time customer intelligence and data from your customers to help you detect the best influencers who are popular among your niche market.

FameBit

A handy tool which lets you connect directly with influencers who are on the lookout for new campaign opportunities. Once you've set up your campaign type on this tool (narrowing down your factors and budget), you'll be able to get to work quickly connecting with influencers who are going to be the right fit for what you need.

Best Tools for Instagram Hashtag Researching

Hashtags are as much a part of the Instagram world as having visuals are. Without a hashtag, your post might look almost naked and incomplete on your profile. That's how much users have become accustomed to seeing hashtags on this social media site. To make your hashtag research a little bit easier, use the following tools to help you out:

Autohash

A tool which is offered free but with in-app purchases for additional features. This is an Android-based app though, and it will help you locate the relevant hashtags on Instagram for your business. Using artificial intelligence technology, Autohash will review the images on your profile, detect the objects within that image, and then proceed to suggest which hashtags might be the most relevant to your content. You also have the option of adding some of the popular hashtags to your clipboard to be used later on.

Display Purposes

Another free tool which helps you locate the perfect hashtag(s) for your profile. This web-based platform works by helping you out with the research portion of it and provides you with the relevant hashtags for your profile content. Simply start by keying in a keyword or a hashtag, and Display Purposes will suggest even more hashtags for you to choose from.

Focal Mark

Another tool which comes for free, but has in-app purchases which means you might have to be willing to spend on certain features. This one works well on both Android and iOS, and it helps you out by choosing which hashtags are going to work best for your profile. Focal Mark works by using an algorithm which takes the photo's subject, location, and the camera which was used to capture that content. It then helps you detect the most popular hashtags which would be the most relevant to your content.

TopTager

Who doesn't love free tools? Marketers will love this one because not only does it display all the most popular and trending hashtags in real time, it also helps you find the hashtags which will be the best match for your keywords. TopTager uses the copy-and-paste function, a simple solution for you to quickly cut and paste the popular hashtags you want to use and put them on your posts.

Instagram Linking Tools

Want to create an effective link on your bio? You can with these tools:

LinkTree

The perfect tool for all your bio linking strategy needs. Why? Because it helps you manage the bio link on your Instagram for you. If you've worked with Instagram for a while, you'll know that you can only put one link on your bio at any given time. Therefore, whenever you want to change it depending on the promotions, special deals, or blog posts which are trending at the moment for your business, it can be a rather cumbersome process to keep manually changing it. Enter LinkTree, to solve all your problems. This tool works by providing your audience with a link which leads them directly to a landing page, where they will find different sections they can click on.

Soldsie

This tool is pretty steep cost-wise because the price would depend on the number of clicks which your link gets. Soldsie caters more towards publications and online retail stores.

Photo-Editing Tools You Need

This is probably among the most important and essential tools you need since Instagram relies heavily on visuals. Here are some of the best photo-editing tools out there for Instagram to give your profile that extra oomph:

Afterlight 2

An all-in-one tool for all your photo editing needs, Afterlight 2 can quickly become a favorite because of all the filters, frames, and typography options that it presents you with. The array of choices help you pick the best ones that will make an impact on your images. You even have the option of creating your own filters with this one!

Enlight

Looking to turn your visuals into the work of art that it is? Enlight will help you out with this one.

Facetune

 For the images that need a little help and touching up, Facetune is here to save the day. If you're not keen on fancy editing programs like Photoshop, this one might do the trick, although it is more suitable for photos with apparel products.

Photoshop Express

A longtime favorite, Photoshop Express has a wide array of features to help take your images one step further. Anything from cropping, text tools, exposure corrections, perspective corrections, blemish removal, filters and border additions, this tool is here to satisfy all your photo editing needs. And for free, too.

Conclusion

In all of the above, I've presented you with some of the better known and almost undoubtedly unknown tips and tricks to increase your numbers of followers on Instagram. As I mentioned at the start, many of these are used by social media marketing firms to do the same thing, and the only difference being: they will charge you a small fortune to achieve what you can do yourself for very little outlay.

A couple of times I mentioned automated software, and I purposely didn't go into too much depth because you might be tempted to skip the tips and jump directly to the software (hoping you could do all of the above, more easily). Unfortunately, increasing followers does take some work early on, at least until you beginning organically growing the numbers of followers. This software only simplifies things once everything has been set up.

I do know the above techniques work because I've tried and tested them all. I'm hoping they'll have the same amount of success for you when you execute them on an ongoing basis.

www.ingramcontent.com/pod-product-compliance
Lightning Source LLC
LaVergne TN
LVHW022313060326
832902LV00020B/3446

* 9 7 8 1 9 8 9 9 6 5 8 4 9 *